Reptiles

Children's Nature Library

HTS BOOKS
AN IMPRINT OF FOREST HOUSE™
School & Library Edition

Louis Weber, C.E.O.
Publications International, Ltd.
7373 North Cicero Avenue
Lincolnwood, Illinois 60646

Printed in U.S.A.

8 7 6 5 4 3 2 1

ISBN 0-88176-596-1

Written by Eileen Spinelli

Credits:
Animals/Animals: M. Austerman: 8; Anthony Bannister: 27; Hans & Judy Beste: 11; M.A. Chappell: 31, 64; John Chellman: 23, 51; Ken Cole: 46; Bruce Davidson: 12, 32; E.R. Degginger: Front Cover, 1, 10, 24, 42; Jim Doran: 58; Michael Fogden: 36; George H.H. Huey: 42, 52; Breck P. Kent: 20, 21, 28, 60; Richard Kolar: 46; J & C Kroeger: 50; Richard K. LaVal: 52; Zig Leszczynski: 7, 9, 14, 17, 26, 34, 35, 43, 48, 60, 61; Bates Littlehales: 29; C.C. Lockwood: 24, 26, 54; Joe McDonald: 44, 45; Raymond A. Mendez: 52, 53; John Nees: 22; Alan G. Nelson: 12; Oxford Scientific Films: Stephen Dalton: 10; Michael Fogden: Back Cover; Alastair Macewen: 10; Godfrey Merlen: 20; LLT Rhodes: 22; Frank Roberts: 18; J.C. Stevenson: 28; Fred Whitehead: 48; **Daniel Lee Brown:** 14; **Ellis Wildlife Collection:** 8, 12, 16, 30, 32, 56; **Clayton Fogle:** 4; **International Stock Photography, Ltd.:** George Ancona: 40; J.G. Edmanson: 6; Tom & Michelle Grimm: 55; Maratea: 57; Lindsay Silverman: 50; J. Robert Stottlemyer: 4; Bill Thomas: 44, 59; **Steven C. Kaufman:** 13, 18, 37, 41, 54; **Tom Stack & Associates:** John Cancalosi: 62, 63; Mary Clay: 39; Christopher Crowley: 47; Brian Parker: 5; Tom Stack: 38; **Vireo:** Doug Wechsler: 25, 30, 40; **Yogi:** R.Y. Kaufman: 3, 6, 15, 19, 33, 34, 49, 58.

Table of Contents

Introduction

The early relatives of the reptiles were the dinosaurs. These big creatures lived millions of years ago. The name dinosaur means "terrible lizard," but not all dinosaurs were big and terrible. Some dinosaurs were as small as dogs, and some were as harmless as chickens.

Today's reptiles are not as big as the brontosaurus or as strong as the powerful Tyrannosaurus rex, but they are just as interesting.

A model of a dinosaur, the Stegasaurus. ▶

Introduction

Reptiles come in all colors, shapes, and sizes. They are covered with scales, and they breathe air. They are cold-blooded animals.

Cold-blooded does not mean their blood is really cold. It means their body heat changes with the air. If the air is warm, the reptile will be warm. If the air is chilly, the reptile will be chilly.

In cold weather, many find a warm place to stay. Some sleep all winter long. Others live in warm places, such as the desert.

Lizards

Many lizards look fierce, but most of these reptiles are harmless. Some lizards are tiny enough to ride on your finger. Others are big enough to give you a ride.

Lizards are covered with scales, which sometimes are as brightly colored as balloons. Some lizards have amazing skin pouches that they can suddenly inflate to scare away enemies.

Lizards can do many different things. Some seem to fly; some walk on water; some run upside down across ceilings; and some even change colors. Lizards are usually good swimmers, but most live on land.

Lizards

The lizard has a strange tongue. It flicks in and out, "tasting" the air. The tongue helps the lizard find food. Lizards like to eat insects.

Lizards keep growing as long as they live. They shed their skin, like snakes do. But unlike snakes, lizards do not shed their skin in one piece. A lizard's skin falls off in small bits.

Most baby lizards hatch from eggs. Baby lizards are smart enough to look after themselves.

Chameleon

The most amazing thing about the chameleon (kuh-MEEL-yuhn) is that this lizard can change colors. That's how it hides. The second most amazing thing about the chameleon is its tongue. Imagine if your tongue were as long as your body! The chameleon's tongue really is as long as its body. This long tongue makes it easy for the chameleon to catch its dinner. What does it like for dinner? Insects, of course!

Horned Toad

Horned toads only look like toads. They're really lizards. They sport an amazing coat of thorns, spikes, and warts. Even though it looks scary, the horned toad is a friendly creature. It rarely bites, but it has a scary defense. When threatened, the horned toad squirts blood from its eyelid. That certainly doesn't invite a closer look! Horned toads like the bright sun. At night and on rainy days, this lizard digs into the sand.

Gecko

The gecko (GEK-o) named itself. When it "talks," it says, "Geck-o...geck-o." This gentle lizard often lives around houses in hot climates. Because it eats annoying insects, it is a most welcome guest. This lizard's feet have sticky pads so it can walk up walls and across ceilings. The gecko's brittle tail breaks off easily. No problem. A new one will grow in its place. Geckos are nighttime animals.

Geckos can walk upside down on walls, just like this one. ▶

Gila Monster

The Gila monster (GEE-lah MAHN-stur) is a lizard with a lovely pink and black beaded coat, so it's often called the beaded lizard. The Gila monster can be fierce. Once it snaps its jaws onto its prey, it is nearly impossible to pry those strong jaws open. And the Gila monster is poisonous, too. During the day, this lizard sleeps underground. The Gila monster stores fat, like a camel does. But the Gila monster stores it in its tail instead of in a hump.

Marine Iguana

The marine iguana (mah-REEN ee-GWAH-nah) lives in the Galápagos Islands in the Pacific Ocean. Of all lizards, the marine iguana is the best swimmer. It often enters the water to eat seaweed. But it likes to sit on sunny rocks just as much. When the marine iguana puffs steam from its nose, just like a storybook dragon, it looks scary. But the marine iguana is really very shy.

Komodo Dragon

The Komodo dragon (ko-MO-do DRA-guhn) is
the biggest lizard of all. This lizard lives on the
island of Komodo in the Indian Ocean. The
Komodo dragon has a long tongue. This tongue
is used more like a nose than a tongue. In other
words, the Komodo dragon smells with its
tongue. The Komodo dragon can climb trees, but
it also likes the ground. It is a rather lazy animal,
especially after dinner.

Snakes

Lots of people are afraid of snakes. Some people won't even touch these reptiles. They think the snake's skin is slimy. But the snake's skin is dry.

Most snakes are not poisonous. Many are shy and would rather slither away from danger than attack.

All snakes can swim, but most live on land. Some live in the desert, some in the mountains. Some snakes have homes underground, some in trees.

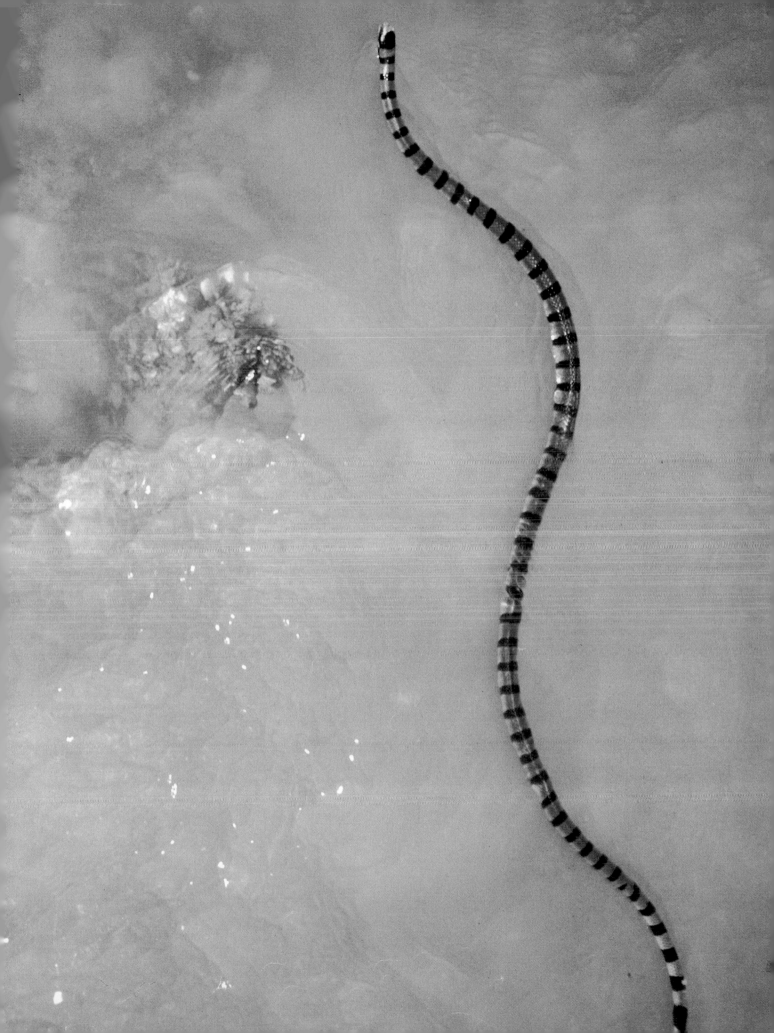

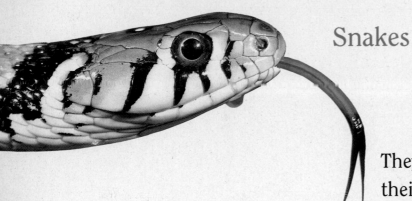

Snakes

Snakes have no legs. They crawl along on their bellies. Snakes have no ears. They hear by feeling vibrations in the ground.

A snake can never shut its eyes because it has no eyelids. Its eyes are always open, but experts think snakes can't see very well. The snake's tongue looks frightening, but it can't hurt you. The snake uses its tongue to smell.

Snakes can eat animals much bigger than themselves. That's because the jaws and ribs of a snake can stretch very wide.

Some baby snakes are born live. Some hatch from eggs. No baby snake needs a mother to care for it.

Garter Snake

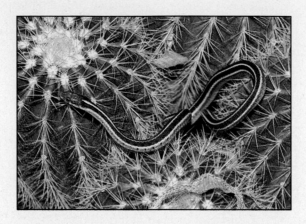

No need to fear the harmless garter snake—unless you happen to be a frog or insect. Then look out! The garter snake might gobble you up.

Garter snakes like to be up and about during the day. Sometimes they nap under porches, rocks, or even city sidewalks. The garter snake is also called the garden snake because it's usually found in gardens. In the winter, the garter snake hibernates.

Boa Constrictor

The boa constrictor (BO-uh kahn-STRIK-tur) is not a poisonous snake. But its sharp teeth can hurt badly. The boa's victims are squeezed.

Because its jaws stretch, the boa can swallow animals bigger than its own head. This snake can be tamed, and many people keep boa constrictors as pets. When tame, this snake will coil itself around your arm and neck. Don't worry—it will not squeeze too hard.

Python

The longest snake in the world is the royal python (PY-thahn). Pythons eat a lot, but they don't eat often. After a big meal, the python might wait a year before eating again. These snakes are good swimmers. They like to wind their bodies around the branches of a tree. Pythons have sharp teeth but no fangs. They are not poisonous. They squeeze their prey.

Rattlesnake

There are many different kinds of rattlesnakes. And every one is poisonous. When a rattler is ready to bite, it coils itself into the shape of the letter S. These are the only snakes that rattle. They make their rattling noise whenever they shake their tails. If you hear such a rattle, better run! Rattlesnakes bite! Even baby rattlesnakes are not safe to handle.

Vipers & Adders

Vipers come in many pretty colors and markings, but they are dangerous snakes. Palm vipers are green. The bushmaster is pink and black.

Vipers are called "pit vipers" because they have holes, or "pits," on their heads. These holes help the viper find its prey.

The adder is a kind of viper called the European viper. You don't want to be bitten by an adder. The adder's bite is poisonous. Sometimes the adder's fangs break off. That's okay; new fangs will replace the old ones.

King Cobra

You have probably seen a picture of a snake dancing up out of a basket to flute music. Many of these dancing snakes are cobras.

The king cobra is fearsome and dangerous. Before it bites, the king cobra flattens and spreads out its neck like a fan. This strange action is called the cobra's hood. It means the cobra is angry. The bite of the king cobra is deadly.

Turtles

The turtle has been made so well that this reptile hasn't changed much since prehistoric times.

The turtle's shell is hard and makes a safe place to hide. When threatened, many turtles

pull themselves into their shells. If you touch a turtle's shell, it will feel it. That's because the shell is covered with a thin layer of skin.

Turtles

Turtles have a good sense of smell. Turtles can see colors, too; most reptiles can't. They do not hear very well, and they are not very "talkative." When frightened, a turtle will make a hissing sound.

Turtles don't have teeth. Many have hard beaks that work just as well.

Not all turtles are slow. In fact, if you picked the wrong turtle to race, you could lose! These fast turtles are the soft-shelled kind.

Some turtles live a long time, longer than any other reptile. Some even live longer than people.

Box Turtle

There are lots of box turtles. They are found in the country. They are also found in the city, usually in parks and vacant lots. Box turtles are harmless and easy to tame. You might be able to tempt one to come closer with a fresh blueberry. When a box turtle is frightened or in danger, it closes its shell up tight. Baby box turtles are about the size of a quarter.

Painted Turtle

The painted turtle isn't really painted. It just has bright, colorful markings. Yellows and reds, splashes and stripes—it is beautiful indeed. Painted turtles are shy. Not around each other, of course, but around people. If a painted turtle were sunning itself on a log and felt you coming, it would plop-splash into the water. Females are bigger than males. Male painted turtles can swim backward in the water.

Snapping Turtle

The snapping turtle doesn't have teeth. But that doesn't mean you should dangle your finger in front of it. The snapping turtle does have powerful, hooked jaws. They snap! This turtle is more dangerous on land than in the water. On land, it will strike if bothered. In water, it swims away from annoyances. The snapping turtle seldom comes to land, except to lay its eggs. A funny thing about its eggs: They're so rubbery that if you drop one, it will bounce!

Galápagos Tortoise

You might see the Galápagos tortoise (guh-LAHP-uh-guhs TORT-uhs) next time you visit the zoo. They are big enough to ride on. In fact, the Galápagos tortoise is the biggest land turtle in the world. This turtle is lazy. It sleeps more than half the day. To keep warm, the Galápagos tortoise covers itself with mud, leaves, or bushes. The Galápagos tortoise lives a long time. One lived to be more than 100 years old.

Leatherback

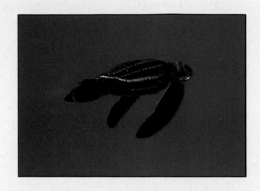 

The leatherback is the biggest living turtle. It can weigh almost as much as a small truck. This turtle spends weeks, even months, at sea. It comes to land only to lay eggs. It usually waits until the moon is up to come ashore. Coming ashore isn't easy for the leatherback mother. This turtle has flippers instead of feet. Flippers are good for swimming, but not for walking on the beach.

Crocodilians

Crocodilians (KRAHK-uh-DIL-ee-uhns) are the biggest and strongest reptiles in the world. The most fearsome crocodilian is the African crocodile.

How can you tell the difference between a crocodile and an alligator? A crocodile's lower teeth jut out, even when its mouth is closed. The alligator's teeth can't be seen unless its mouth is open.

Crocodilians

Crocodilians hate cold weather. They usually live where it's warm.

Crocodilians feel quite at home when almost completely under water. All crocodilians have webbed feet. They also have special plugs called "valves" in their faces that keep water out of the crocodilian's nose and mouth. The eyes are set high on the heads of these creatures.

Baby crocodilians are hatched from eggs.

Alligator

Early stories described the alligator as a huge monster with fire-breath and a roar that shook the ground. But the alligator isn't as mean to other alligators as it looks. A mother alligator often lets her babies ride on her back. And she might make a little swimming hole with her tail for the babies. In winter, alligators are less active.

Crocodile

Crocodiles can be cranky and dangerous. But here is something that is sure to surprise you. Crocodiles make very good mothers!

Crocodiles can't stand the cold. As a matter of fact, if the crocodile's swimming place gets too cold, the crocodile may die.

The Nile crocodile is found in Africa. The American crocodile makes its home in Florida, Central America, and the Caribbean.

Tuatara

The Tuatara (TOO-uh-TAHR-uh) isn't like any other reptile on Earth. It looks like a lizard, but it isn't a lizard. And it's not a snake or turtle or crocodilian either. The tuatara is the same now as it was during the age of dinosaurs.

This animal is very slow. Even its eggs take more than a year to hatch. The tuatara makes a croaking sound, like a frog.

To find a tuatara, you would have to go all the way to New Zealand.

Galápagos tortoise